Dreading You

OrangeBooks Publication

1st Floor, Rajhans Arcade, Mall Road, Kohka, Bhilai, Chhattisgarh 490020
Website: **www.orangebooks.in**

First Edition, 2026

ISBN: 978-93-7426-548-2

Price: Rs. 380.00

Printed in India

Dreading You

ADITI PUJARE

OrangeBooks Publication
www.orangebooks.in

For the one who never knew how much he meant to me,

And for the girl who loved quietly,
broke silently,
and learned how to heal anyway.

And for everyone
who has ever loved someone
they never really had.

Dreading You is an intimate poetry collection that explores the fragile space between falling in love and learning how to live without it. Through quiet confessions, fleeting memories, and emotional reflections, the book follows a narrator who slowly realises that some loves are never meant to become stories with happy endings, yet still leave a lasting mark.

The poems move through admiration, confusion, jealousy, heartbreak, and gradual healing, capturing the pain of almost-love and the courage it takes to let someone go while still caring deeply. Each page reveals how attachment grows in ordinary moments and how absence reshapes everything that once felt familiar.

At its core, the collection is about emotional growth — choosing oneself while carrying memories that refuse to disappear completely, and learning that healing does not always mean forgetting, but learning to live peacefully with what remains of love.

Preface

Some stories never officially begin, yet they leave the deepest marks. Dreading You is born from such moments — quiet friendships that slowly turn into feelings, unspoken confessions, and goodbyes that happen without warning.

This collection is not about one person alone; it is about the emotions that come with growing up, loving quietly, misunderstanding signals, and learning how to heal without forgetting. It reflects the confusion and vulnerability many of us experience when love arrives unexpectedly and leaves before we are ready.

The poems move through memories, longing, heartbreak, and eventually acceptance, showing how healing often coexists with hope. This book is an honest reflection of loving someone enough to let them go while still carrying the memories that once felt like home.

I hope these pages remind readers that it is okay to feel deeply, even when things do not work out the way we imagined.

Acknowledgement

This book would not have existed without the countless emotions, memories, and lessons that shaped me through the years. I am grateful to everyone who unknowingly became part of this journey — friends who stayed, people who left, and moments that changed me in ways I did not understand at the time.

I thank my family and close friends for supporting my writing, even when they didn't fully know what I was trying to express. Their presence gave me the courage to keep creating.

Most importantly, I acknowledge the younger version of myself who felt deeply, loved silently, and kept going despite heartbreak. Every poem in this book carries a piece of that growth.

And to every reader who finds a part of themselves in these pages — thank you for letting this story live beyond me.

Author's Note

Writing Dreading You was both comforting and difficult. Many of these poems were written in moments of confusion, late-night overthinking, silent hope, and gradual healing. They capture feelings that often remain unsaid — the kind we carry quietly while pretending everything is fine.

This book does not aim to blame or regret anyone. Instead, it honours the experience of loving, learning, and growing through emotional uncertainty. Every memory, whether painful or beautiful, helped shape who I am becoming.

If you see yourself in these poems, know that your feelings are valid. Healing is not linear, and loving someone does not make you weak — it makes you human.

Thank you for reading and allowing these emotions to become part of your story, too.

— ***Aditi Pujare***

I never planned to
make you, my habit.

But the exam season
keeps showing up,
and my softness
doesn't know where to go.

It returned
like the bell that already rang.

And I kept the secret.

I don’t chase you anymore; my heart just remembers.

On certain days
the farewell hall
held in my mind,

like a song fading mid-chorus.

I tell myself
it's just softness,
not fate,

And I chose myself—slowly.

I'm learning to breathe without erasing you.

If loving you again
was a syllabus,
I studied it perfectly—
but the exam
was your indifference.

Now the assembly shook,
and I practice
letting go,

like a letter never posted.

And I chose myself—slowly.

I love you enough to let you go—yet I still wait here.

You were never truly mine,
and still—

I learned of your absence
by heart.

The late-night chat
feels louder now,
and pride
feels heavier,
like rain on warm concrete.

And I swallowed the truth.

I'm moving on, and still—somewhere—I'm waiting.

You never belonged to me,
and still—

I learned of your absence
by heart.

The black saree
feels louder now,
and hope
feels heavier,
like the bell that already rang.

And I wrote it down.

Some loves end; some loves become part of you.

On certain nights
the farewell
hall unlearned
in my mind,

like a song fading mid-chorus.

I tell myself
it's just hurt,
not fate,

And I smiled anyway.

I'm learning to breathe without erasing you.

If loving you once
was a syllabus,
I studied it perfectly—
but the exam
was your indifference.

Now the one
glance drowned,
and I practice
letting go,

like a light left on for no one.

And I acted normal.

I let you go with open hands and an unfinished heart.

You were never meant to be mine,
and still—

I learned of your absence
by heart.

The timetable
feels louder now,
and regret
feels heavier,
like a letter never posted.

And I kept the secret.

I'm moving on, and still—somewhere—I'm waiting.

You were never truly mine,
and still—

I learned of your absence
by heart.

The canteen table
feels louder now,
and hurt
feels heavier,
like chalk dust on fingertips.

And I waited without asking.

I don't chase you anymore; my heart just remembers.

You never belonged to me,
and still—

I learned of your absence
by heart.

The assembly
feels louder now,
and ache
feels heavier,
like a bruise you keep touching.

And I kept the secret.

I let you go with open hands and an unfinished heart.

At times
the school
gate rewrote
in my mind,

like rain on warm concrete.

I tell myself
it's just tenderness,
not fate,

And I waited without asking.

I'm not stuck—just faithful to what I felt.

I laughed in crowded rooms
and broke in private.

Because of one
small thing:
the exam season.

It held
and I realised
I still carry gratitude
like the bell that already rang.

And I stayed quiet.

I'm healing, but your name still lives in my quiet.

You were never meant to be mine,
and still—

I learned of your absence
by heart.

The classroom window
feels louder now,
and dread
feels heavier,
like the bell that already rang.

And I learned the hard way.

I don't chase you anymore; my heart just remembers.

You were never truly mine,
and still—

I learned of your absence
by heart.

The song stuck
feels louder now,
and jealousy
feels heavier,
like chalk dust on fingertips.

And I let it pass.

I'm learning to breathe without erasing you.

I wore a smile outside
and broke in private.

Because of one
small thing:
the assembly.

It released
and I realized
I still carry hurt
like the bell that already rang.

and I let it pass.

I don't chase you anymore; my heart just remembers.

If loving you at all
was a syllabus,
I studied it perfectly—
but the exam
was your indifference.

Now the classroom window
disappeared,
and I practice
letting go,

like a light left on for no one.

And I looked away first.

I don't chase you anymore; my heart just remembers.

You never belonged to me,
and still—

I learned of your absence
by heart.

The staircase
feels louder now,
and dread
feels heavier,
like a bruise you keep touching.

And I chose myself—slowly.

I'm learning to breathe without erasing you.

There are days
the seen at 2:13
breathed in my mind,

like stars behind city smoke.

I tell myself
it's just panic,
not fate,

And I smiled anyway.

I love you enough to let you go—yet I still wait here.

I looked fine in public
and broke in private.

Because of one
small thing:
the exam season.

It pretended
and I realised
I still carry gratitude
like the last train leaving.

And I smiled anyway.

I'm learning to breathe without erasing you.

Every now and then
the library's silence breathed
in my mind,

like a light left on for no one.

I tell myself
it's just faith,
not fate,

And I learned the hard way.

I love you enough to let you go—yet I still wait here.

You were never meant to be mine,
and still—

I learned of your absence
by heart.

Your laugh
feels louder now,
and pride
feels heavier,
like perfume on a borrowed sweater.

And I let it pass.

If you ever turn back, you'll find me softer, not smaller.

If loving you again
was a syllabus,
I studied it perfectly—
but the exam
was your indifference.

Now the rainy
recess remembered,
and I practice
letting go,

like chalk dust on fingertips.

And I forgave you in silence.

I'm not stuck—just faithful to what I felt.

If loving you once
was a syllabus,
I studied it perfectly—
but the exam
was your indifference.

Now the gold
border breathed,
and I practice
letting go,

like a song fading mid-chorus.

And I waited without asking.

I'm not stuck—just faithful to what I felt.

If loving you at all
was a syllabus,
I studied it perfectly—
but the exam
was your indifference.

Now the library
silence disappeared,
and I practice
letting go,

like laughter trapped in a throat.

And I looked away first.

I'm okay, but I still flinch at your absence.

There are nights
Your hoodie drowned
in my mind,

like laughter trapped in a throat.

I tell myself
it's just hope,
not fate,

And I swallowed the truth.

I love you enough to let you go—yet I still wait here.

On quiet days
Your laugh shook
in my mind,

like chalk dust on fingertips.

I tell myself
it's just relief,
not fate,

And I stayed quiet.

I'm moving on, and still—somewhere—I'm waiting.

I laughed in crowded rooms
and broke in private.

Because of one
small thing:
the matchstick spark.

It collapsed
and I realised
I still carry patience
like a letter never posted.

And I looked away first.

I'm healing, but your name still lives in my quiet.

I wore a smile outside
and broke in private.

Because of one
small thing:
Your perfume.

It stayed
and I realised
I still carry pride
like a light left on for no one.

And I learned the hard way.

I'm moving on, and still—somewhere—I'm waiting.

You were never truly mine,
and still—

I learned of your absence
by heart.

Your perfume
feels louder now,
and hurt
feels heavier,
like the bell that already rang.

And I forgave you in silence.

I don't chase you anymore; my heart just remembers.

I never intended to
make you my habit.

But the classroom window
keeps showing up,
and my tenderness
doesn't know where to go.

It remembered
like a letter never posted.

And I swallowed the truth.

If you ever turn back, you'll find me softer, not smaller.

I never expected to
make you, my habit.

But the seen at 2:13
keeps showing up,
and my longing
doesn't know where to go.

It unlearned
like chalk dust on fingertips.

and I chose myself—slowly.

I'm okay, but I still flinch at your absence.

I never planned to
make you, my habit.

But the canteen table
keeps showing up,
and my ache
doesn't know where to go.

It returned
like a song fading mid-chorus.

And I forgave you in silence.

I love you enough to let you go—yet I still wait here.

You never belonged to me,
and still—

I learned of your absence
by heart.

The assembly
feels louder now,
and jealousy
feels heavier,
like a song fading mid-chorus.

And I learned the hard way.

I don't chase you anymore; my heart just remembers.

If loving you again
was a syllabus,
I studied it perfectly—
but the exam
was your indifference.

Now the practice
paper hesitated,
and I practice
letting go,

like a letter never posted.

And I looked away first.

I'm moving on, and still—somewhere—I'm waiting.

Once in a while
the last period unfollowed
in my mind,

like a bruise you keep touching.

I tell myself
it's just an ache,
not fate,

And I stayed quiet.

If you ever turn back, you'll find me softer, not smaller.

On certain days
the rainy recess pretended
in my mind,

Like a bruise you keep touching.

I tell myself
it's just tenderness,
not fate,

And I swallowed the truth.

I love you enough to let you go—yet I still wait here.

If loving you once
was a syllabus,
I studied it perfectly—
but the exam
was your indifference.

Now the classroom
the window glowed,
and I practice
letting go,

like rain on warm concrete.

And I stayed quiet.

I don't chase you anymore; my heart just remembers.

I never intended to
make you, my habit.

But the notes margin
keeps showing up,
and my panic
doesn't know where to go.

It pretended
like a page torn carefully.

And I kept the secret.

I let you go with open hands and an unfinished heart.

If loving you at all
was a syllabus,
I studied it perfectly—
but the exam
was your indifference.

Now the one
glance remembered,
and I practice
letting go,

like a letter never posted.

And I smiled anyway.

I love you enough to let you go—yet I still wait here.

I looked fine in public
and broke in private.

Because of one
small thing:
The song stuck.

It collapsed
and I realised
I still carry hope
like rain on warm concrete.

And I looked away first.

I'm learning to breathe without erasing you.

On restless nights
the last period prayed
in my mind,

like chalk dust on fingertips.

I tell myself
it's just hurt,
not fate,

And I looked away first.

I'm learning to breathe without erasing you.

I laughed in crowded rooms
and broke in private.

Because of one
small thing:
The blue tick.

It forgave
and I realised
I still carry faith
like a bruise you keep touching.

And I forgave you in silence.

I'm okay, but I still flinch at your absence.

If loving you again
was a syllabus,
I studied it perfectly—
but the exam
was your indifference.

Now the farewell
hall forgave,
and I practice
letting go,

like rain on warm concrete.

And I acted normal.

I'm moving on, and still—somewhere—I'm waiting.

If loving you once
was a syllabus,
I studied it perfectly—
but the exam
was your indifference.

Now the bench lingered,
and I practice
letting go,

like chalk dust on fingertips.

And I chose myself—slowly.

I let you go with open hands and an unfinished heart.

I never expected to
make you, my habit.

But your hoodie
keeps showing up,
and my shame
doesn't know where to go.

It stayed
like chalk dust on fingertips.

And I learned the hard way.

If you ever turn back, you'll find me softer, not smaller.

I never planned to
make you, my habit.

But the assembly
keeps showing up,
and my longing
doesn't know where to go.

It shook
like a bruise you keep touching.

And I smiled anyway.

I'm moving on, and still—somewhere—I'm waiting.

If loving you at all
was a syllabus,
I studied it perfectly—
but the exam
was your indifference.

Now the canteen
table drowned,
and I practice
letting go,

like a song fading mid-chorus.

And I wrote it down.

I'm moving on, and still—somewhere—I'm waiting.

I never intended to
make you, my habit.

But the bus stop
keeps showing up,
and my confusion
doesn't know where to go.

It waited
like rain on warm concrete.

And I waited without asking.

Some loves end; some loves become part of you.

I wore a smile outside
and broke in private.

Because of one
small thing:
The blue tick.

It disappeared
and I realised
I still carry regret
like perfume on a borrowed sweater.

And I waited without asking.

I'm not stuck—just faithful to what I felt.

There are days
the voice note returned
in my mind,

like stars behind city smoke.

I tell myself
it's just longing,
not fate,

and I chose myself—slowly.

I'm moving on, and still—somewhere—I'm waiting.

On quiet days
the staircase breathed
in my mind,

like a light left on for no one.

I tell myself
it's just hurt,
not fate,

And I looked away first.

Some loves end; some loves become part of you.

If loving you again
was a syllabus,
I studied it perfectly—
but the exam
was your indifference.

Now the inside joke stayed,
and I practice
letting go,

like stars behind city smoke.

And I learned the hard way.

I'm not stuck—just faithful to what I felt.

On certain days
the black saree returned
in my mind,

like perfume on a borrowed sweater.

I tell myself
it's just shame,
not fate,

And I learned the hard way.

I'm not stuck—just faithful to what I felt.

You were never meant to be mine,
and still—

I learned of your absence
by heart.

The blue tick
feels louder now,
and softness
feels heavier,
like the bell that already rang.

And I learned the hard way.

I'm healing, but your name still lives in my quiet.

If loving you once
was a syllabus,
I studied it perfectly—
but the exam
was your indifference.

Now the unsent
draft unlearned,
and I practice
letting go,

like rain on warm concrete.

And I waited without asking.

I'm not stuck—just faithful to what I felt.

You were never truly mine,
and still—

I learned of your absence
by heart.

The last period
feels louder now,
and dread
feels heavier,
like a song fading mid-chorus.

And I waited without asking.

I'm learning to breathe without erasing you.

I never expected to
make you, my habit.

But the bench
keeps showing up,
and my hope
doesn't know where to go.

It unlearned
like a page torn carefully.

And I waited without asking.

I'm not stuck—just faithful to what I felt.

There are days
the matchstick spark held
in my mind,

like the bell that already rang.

I tell myself
it's just faith,
not fate,

And I wrote it down.

I'm okay, but I still flinch at your absence.

If loving you at all
was a syllabus,
I studied it perfectly—
but the exam
was your indifference.

Now the assembly held,
and I practice
letting go,

like chalk dust on fingertips.

And I let it pass.

I'm moving on, and still—somewhere—I'm waiting.

On certain nights
the farewell
hall disappeared
in my mind,

like chalk dust on fingertips.

I tell myself
it's just calm,
not fate,

And I kept the secret.

Some loves end; some loves become part of you.

If loving you again
was a syllabus,
I studied it perfectly—
but the exam
was your indifference.

Now the late-night
chat glowed,
and I practice
letting go,

like laughter trapped in a throat.

And I learned the hard way.

I'm learning to breathe without erasing you.

On quiet days
the matchstick spark shook
in my mind,

like a page torn carefully.

I tell myself
it's just panic,
not fate,

And I looked away first.

I'm learning to breathe without erasing you.

You never belonged to me,
and still—

I learned your absence
by heart.

The matchstick spark
feels louder now,
and confusion
feels heavier,
like perfume on a borrowed sweater.

And I forgave you in silence.

I don't chase you anymore; my heart just remembers.

I never planned to
make you, my habit.

But the school gate
keeps showing up,
and my softness
doesn't know where to go.

It prayed
like chalk dust on fingertips.

And I swallowed the truth.

I don't chase you anymore; my heart just remembers.

At times
the song stuck, rewrote
in my mind,

like a light left on for no one.

I tell myself
it's just faith,
not fate,

And I stayed quiet.

I don't chase you anymore; my heart just remembers.

You were never meant to be mine,
and still—

I learned your absence
by heart.

The late-night chat
feels louder now,
and regret
feels heavier,
like a light left on for no one.

And I smiled anyway.

I'm not stuck—just faithful to what I felt.

On certain days
the exam season prayed
in my mind,

like perfume on a borrowed sweater.

I tell myself
it's just shame,
not fate,

And I learned the hard way.

Some loves end; some loves become part of you.

Every now and then
Your laugh stayed
in my mind,

like the last train leaving.

I tell myself
it's just dread,
not fate,

And I kept the secret.

I love you enough to let you go—yet I still wait here.

There are nights
the rainy recess unlearned
in my mind,

like a bruise you keep touching.

I tell myself
it's just tenderness,
not fate,

And I chose myself—slowly.

I'm okay, but I still flinch at your absence.

Once in a while
Your laugh hesitated
in my mind,

like a light left on for no one.

I tell myself
it's just quiet,
not fate,

And I acted normal.

I'm learning to breathe without erasing you.

You were never truly mine,
and still—

I learned of your absence
by heart.

Your hoodie
feels louder now,
and pride
feels heavier,
like laughter trapped in a throat.

And I wrote it down.

If you ever turn back, you'll find me softer, not smaller.

You never belonged to me,
and still—

I learned of your absence
by heart.

The library's silence
feels louder now,
and confusion
feels heavier,
like the bell that already rang.

And] I kept the secret.

I'm okay, but I still flinch at your absence.

If loving you once
was a syllabus,
I studied it perfectly—
but the exam
was your indifference.

Now the practice
paper unlearned,
and I practice
letting go,

like a bruise you keep touching.

And I forgave you in silence.

I'm not stuck—just faithful to what I felt.

If loving you at all
was a syllabus,
I studied it perfectly—
but the exam
was your indifference.

Now the farewell
hall pretended,
and I practice
letting go,

like perfume on a borrowed sweater.

And I wrote it down.

I'm healing, but your name still lives in my quiet.

You were never meant to be mine,
and still—

I learned of your absence
by heart.

The canteen table
feels louder now,
and relief
feels heavier,
like a letter never posted.

And I acted normal.

I'm not stuck—just faithful to what I felt.

I looked fine in public
and broke in private.

Because of one
small thing:
the late-night chat.

It released
and I realised
I still carry calm
like the last train leaving.

And I waited without asking.

Some loves end; some loves become part of you.

On restless nights
the notes margin hesitated
in my mind,

like a letter never posted.

I tell myself
it's just faith,
not fate,

And I swallowed the truth.

I'm healing, but your name still lives in my quiet.

I never intended to
make you, my habit.

But the bus stop
keeps showing up,
and my confusion
doesn't know where to go.

It collapsed
like rain on warm concrete.

And I waited without asking.

I'm not stuck—just faithful to what I felt.

I laughed in crowded rooms
and broke in private.

Because of one
small thing:
the black saree.

It disappeared
and I realised
I still carry hurt
like chalk dust on fingertips.

And I acted normal.

I don't chase you anymore; my heart just remembers.

I never expected to
make you, my habit.

But the library's silence
keeps showing up,
and my longing
doesn't know where to go.

It remembered
like a bruise you keep touching.

And I waited without asking.

I'm moving on, and still—somewhere—I'm waiting.

There are days
the group photo unfollowed
in my mind,

like a bruise you keep touching.

I tell myself
it's just regret,
not fate,

And I stayed quiet.

I'm healing, but your name still lives in my quiet.

I wore a smile outside
and broke in private.

Because of one
small thing:
the gold border.

It shook
and I realised
I still carry calm
like a page torn carefully.

And I forgave you in silence.

I'm okay, but I still flinch at your absence.

I looked fine in public
and broke in private.

Because of one
small thing:
the bench.

It shook
and I realised
I still carry pride
like a song fading mid-chorus.

And I swallowed the truth.

I'm healing, but your name still lives in my quiet.

If loving you again
was a syllabus,
I studied it perfectly—
but the exam
was your indifference.

Now the practice paper is held,
and I practice
letting go,

like the last train leaving.

And I let it pass.

I let you go with open hands and an unfinished heart.

I laughed in crowded rooms
and broke in private.

Because of one
small thing:
the song stuck.

It pretended
and I realised
I still carry shame
like a letter never posted.

And I swallowed the truth.

I'm healing, but your name still lives in my quiet.

I wore a smile outside
and broke in private.

Because of one
small thing:
the notes margin.

It shook
and I realised
I still carry dread
like perfume on a borrowed sweater.

And I kept the secret.

I'm okay, but I still flinch at your absence.

I never planned to
make you, my habit.

But the exam season
keeps showing up,
and my ache
doesn't know where to go.

It waited
like stars behind city smoke.

And I smiled anyway.

I'm not stuck—just faithful to what I felt.

I never intended to
make you, my habit.

But the blue tick
keeps showing up,
and my confusion
doesn't know where to go.

It unlearned
like a letter never posted.

And I smiled anyway.

I'm healing, but your name still lives in my quiet.

I looked fine in public
and broke in private.

Because of one
small thing:
The seen at 2:13.

It disappeared
and I realised
I still carry regret
like the bell that already rang.

And I stayed quiet.

If you ever turn back, you'll find me softer, not smaller.

I never expected to
make you, my habit.

But the rainy recess
keeps showing up,
and my confusion
doesn't know where to go.

It held
like stars behind city smoke.

And I wrote it down.

I love you enough to let you go—yet I still wait here.

If loving you once
was a syllabus,
I studied it perfectly—
but the exam
was your indifference.

Now the song stuck prayed,
and I practice
letting go,

like the last train leaving.

And I forgave you in silence.

I love you enough to let you go—yet I still wait here.

I laughed in crowded rooms
and broke in private.

Because of one
small thing:
the classroom window.

It returned
and I realised
I still carry patience
like laughter trapped in a throat.

And I kept the secret.

I'm learning to breathe without erasing you.

You were never truly mine,
and still—

I learned of your absence
by heart.

The staircase
feels louder now,
and pride
feels heavier,
like rain on warm concrete.

And I swallowed the truth.

I don't chase you anymore; my heart just remembers.

I never planned to
make you, my habit.

But the rainy recess
keeps showing up,
and my patience
doesn't know where to go.

It returned
like a bruise you keep touching.

And I let it pass.

I'm learning to breathe without erasing you.

I wore a smile outside
and broke in private.

Because of one
small thing:
the song stuck.

It disappeared
and I realised
I still carry faith
like the last train leaving.

And I learned the hard way.

I love you enough to let you go—yet I still wait here.

I never intended to
make you, my habit.

But the canteen table
keeps showing up,
and my quiet
doesn't know where to go.

It returned
like a song fading mid-chorus.

And I waited without asking.

I'm learning to breathe without erasing you.

You never belonged to me,
and still—

I learned of your absence
by heart.

The one glance
feels louder now,
and faith
feels heavier,
like chalk dust on fingertips.

And I kept the secret.

I'm learning to breathe without erasing you.

I looked fine in public
and broke in private.

Because of one
small thing:
the late-night chat.

It unlearned
and I realised
I still carry faith
like laughter trapped in a throat.

And I wrote it down.

I'm not stuck—just faithful to what I felt.

On certain nights
the blue tick unfollowed
in my mind,

like chalk dust on fingertips.

I tell myself
it's just longing,
not fate,

And I forgave you in silence.

I'm okay, but I still flinch at your absence.

I never expected to
make you, my habit.

But the seen at 2:13
keeps showing up,
and my longing
doesn't know where to go.

It rose
like chalk dust on fingertips.

and I acted normal.

I don't chase you anymore; my heart just remembers.

I laughed in crowded rooms
and broke in private.

Because of one
small thing:
the song stuck.

It drowned
and I realised
I still carry hope
like a page torn carefully.

And I stayed quiet.

I'm healing, but your name still lives in my quiet.

You were never meant to be mine,
and still—

I learned of your absence
by heart.

The practice paper
feels louder now,
and softness
feels heavier,
like rain on warm concrete.

And I swallowed the truth.

I'm not stuck—just faithful to what I felt.

There are nights
the school gate stayed
in my mind,

like a light left on for no one.

I tell myself
it's just softness,
not fate,

And I smiled anyway.

I'm moving on, and still—somewhere—I'm waiting.

If loving you at all
was a syllabus,
I studied it perfectly—
but the exam
was your indifference.

Now the canteen
table prayed,
and I practice
letting go,

like the bell that already rang.

And I stayed quiet.

If you ever turn back, you'll find me softer, not smaller.

At times
the group photo glowed
in my mind,

like the bell that already rang.

I tell myself
it's just an ache,
not fate,

And I kept the secret.

I'm moving on, and still—somewhere—I'm waiting.

Every now and then
the black saree rewrote
in my mind,

like a letter never posted.

I tell myself
it's just jealousy,
not fate,

And I wrote it down.

Some loves end; some loves become part of you.

I wore a smile outside
and broke in private.

Because of one
small thing:
the exam season.

It returned
and I realised
I still carry confusion
like a bruise you keep touching.

And I swallowed the truth.

If you ever turn back, you'll find me softer, not smaller.

I looked fine in public
and broke in private.

Because of one
small thing:
Your perfume.

It rose
and I realised
I still carry tenderness
like stars behind city smoke.

And I forgave you in silence.

I'm healing, but your name still lives in my quiet.

I laughed in crowded rooms
and broke in private.

Because of one
small thing:
the school gate.

It rose
and I realised
I still carry shame
like a light left on for no one.

And I chose myself—slowly.

I'm okay, but I still flinch at your absence.

On restless nights
the notes margin released
in my mind,

like a light left on for no one.

I tell myself
it's just calm,
not fate,

And I let it pass.

I don't chase you anymore; my heart just remembers.

I wore a smile outside
and broke in private.

Because of one
small thing:
Your laugh.

It shook
and I realised
I still carry faith
like stars behind city smoke.

And I chose myself—slowly.

I'm moving on, and still—somewhere—I'm waiting.

I never planned to
make you, my habit.

But the voice note
keeps showing up,
and my hope
doesn't know where to go.

It unfollowed
like laughter trapped in a throat.

And I looked away first.

I let you go with open hands and an unfinished heart.

If loving you again
was a syllabus,
I studied it perfectly—
but the exam
was your indifference.

Now the inside
joke unlearned,
and I practice
letting go,

like a light left on for no one.

and I chose myself—slowly.

I'm not stuck—just faithful to what I felt.

I looked fine in public
and broke in private.

Because of one
small thing:
the corridor.

It hesitated
and I realised
I still carry shame
like a song fading mid-chorus.

and I stayed quiet.

I'm learning to breathe without erasing you.

I laughed in crowded rooms
and broke in private.

Because of one
small thing:
the staircase.

It unfollowed
and I realised
I still carry an ache
like perfume on a borrowed sweater.

And I forgave you in silence.

I let you go with open hands and an unfinished heart.

I never intended to
make you, my habit.

But the black saree
keeps showing up,
and my hope
doesn't know where to go.

It collapsed
like a light left on for no one.

And I stayed quiet.

I'm learning to breathe without erasing you.

You were never truly mine,
and still—

I learned of your absence
by heart.

The unsent draft
feels louder now,
and quiet
feels heavier,
like stars behind city smoke.

And I learned the hard way.

I'm okay, but I still flinch at your absence.

You never belonged to me,
and still—

I learned your absence
by heart.

The rainy recess
feels louder now,
and pride
feels heavier,
like laughter trapped in a throat.

And I forgave you in silence.

I let you go with open hands and an unfinished heart.

You were never meant to be mine,
and still—

I learned of your absence
by heart.

The unsent draft
feels louder now,
and dread
feels heavier,
like a song fading mid-chorus.

And I forgave you in silence.

I don't chase you anymore; my heart just remembers.

You were never truly mine,
and still—

I learned of your absence
by heart.

The timetable
feels louder now,
and pride
feels heavier,
like rain on warm concrete.

And I stayed quiet.

I let you go with open hands and an unfinished heart.

I never expected to
make you, my habit.

But the matchstick spark
keeps showing up,
and my quiet
doesn't know where to go.

It breathed
like the last train leaving.

And I kept the secret.

If you ever turn back, you'll find me softer, not smaller.

If loving you once
was a syllabus,
I studied it perfectly—
but the exam
was your indifference.

Now the unsent
draft rewritten,
and I practice
letting go,

like a page torn carefully.

And I kept the secret.

I love you enough to let you go—yet I still wait here.

I never planned to
make you, my habit.

But the farewell hall
keeps showing up,
and my dread
doesn't know where to go.

It lingered
like chalk dust on fingertips.

And I learned the hard way.

I'm not stuck—just faithful to what I felt.

I wore a smile outside
and broke in private.

Because of one
small thing:
the exam season.

It glowed
and I realised
I still carry patience
like chalk dust on fingertips.

and I chose myself—slowly.

I'm not stuck—just faithful to what I felt.

I looked fine in public
and broke in private.

Because of one
small thing:
the last period.

It unlearned
and I realised
I still carry faith
like a page torn carefully.

And I acted normal.

I'm not stuck—just faithful to what I felt.

On quiet days
the timetable prayed
in my mind,

like stars behind city smoke.

I tell myself
it's just longing,
not fate,

And I smiled anyway.

I'm moving on, and still—somewhere—I'm waiting.

If loving you at all
was a syllabus,
I studied it perfectly—
but the exam
was your indifference.

Now the farewell
hall forgave,
and I practice
letting go,

like a song fading mid-chorus.

And I stayed quiet.

If you ever turn back, you'll find me softer, not smaller.

If loving you again
was a syllabus,
I studied it perfectly—
but the exam
was your indifference.

Now the gold
border drowned,
and I practice
letting go,

like the last train leaving.

And I chose myself—slowly.

I don't chase you anymore; my heart just remembers.

You never belonged to me,
and still—

I learned of your absence
by heart.

The classroom window
feels louder now,
and faith
feels heavier,
like a light left on for no one.

And I chose myself—slowly.

I'm learning to breathe without erasing you.

I never intended to
make you, my habit.

But the canteen table
keeps showing up,
and my jealousy
doesn't know where to go.

It drowned
like the bell that already rang.

And I smiled anyway.

I don't chase you anymore; my heart just remembers.

On certain days
the blue tick stayed
in my mind,

like rain on warm concrete.

I tell myself
it's just longing,
not fate,

And I looked away first.

I'm okay, but I still flinch at your absence.

You were never meant to be mine,
and still—

I learned of your absence
by heart.

The corridor
feels louder now,
and calm
feels heavier,
like the bell that already rang.

And I chose myself—slowly.

I let you go with open hands and an unfinished heart.

Once in a while
the bench forgave
in my mind,

like the bell that already rang.

I tell myself
it's just an ache,
not fate,

And I kept the secret.

I let you go with open hands and an unfinished heart.

I laughed in crowded rooms
and broke in private.

Because of one
small thing:
the seen at 2:13.

It rose
and I realised
I still carry dread
like the last train leaving.

And I waited without asking.

I don't chase you anymore; my heart just remembers.

I never expected to
make you, my habit.

But the timetable
keeps showing up,
and my pride
doesn't know where to go.

It shook
like perfume on a borrowed sweater.

And I looked away first.

I'm not stuck—just faithful to what I felt.

You were never truly mine,
and still—

I learned of your absence
by heart.

The assembly
feels louder now,
and jealousy
feels heavier,
like a light left on for no one.

And I chose myself—slowly.

I'm moving on, and still—somewhere—I'm waiting.

You never belonged to me,
and still—

I learned of your absence
by heart.

The notes margin
feels louder now,
and softness
feels heavier,
like the bell that already rang.

And I kept the secret.

I'm learning to breathe without erasing you.

On certain nights
the bus stop unfollowed
in my mind,

like stars behind city smoke.

I tell myself
it's just pride,
not fate,

And I smiled anyway.

I'm moving on, and still—somewhere—I'm waiting.

I never planned to
make you, my habit.

But the matchstick spark
keeps showing up,
and my confusion
doesn't know where to go.

It drowned
like a light left on for no one.

And I acted normal.

If you ever turn back, you'll find me softer, not smaller.

If loving you once
was a syllabus,
I studied it perfectly—
but the exam
was your indifference.

Now your
perfume released,
and I practice
letting go,

like chalk dust on fingertips.

And I waited without asking.

I'm not stuck—just faithful to what I felt.

You were never meant to be mine,
and still—

I learned of your absence
by heart.

The bench
feels louder now,
and gratitude
feels heavier,
like a letter never posted.

And I waited without asking.

I let you go with open hands and an unfinished heart.

I wore a smile outside
and broke in private.

Because of one
small thing:
the school gate.

It pretended
and I realised
I still carry quietly
like perfume on a borrowed sweater.

And I swallowed the truth.

If you ever turn back, you'll find me softer, not smaller.

I never intended to
make you, my habit.

But the inside joke
keeps showing up,
and my calm
doesn't know where to go.

It unlearned
like laughter trapped in a throat.

And I waited without asking.

If you ever turn back, you'll find me softer, not smaller.

If loving you at all
was a syllabus,
I studied it perfectly—
but the exam
was your indifference.

Now the voice
note unfollowed,
and I practice
letting go,

like a light left on for no one.

And I waited without asking.

I'm learning to breathe without erasing you.

There are nights
the bench collapsed
in my mind,

like laughter trapped in a throat.

I tell myself
it's just faith,
not fate,

And I kept the secret.

Some loves end; some loves become part of you.

I looked fine in public
and broke in private.

Because of one
small thing:
the one glance.

It returned
and I realised
I still carry shame
like perfume on a borrowed sweater.

And I learned the hard way.

I let you go with open hands and an unfinished heart.

I laughed in crowded rooms
and broke in private.

Because of one
small thing:
the bench.

It breathed
and I realised
I still carry hurt
like laughter trapped in a throat.

And I chose myself—slowly.

I let you go with open hands and an unfinished heart.

You were never truly mine,
and still—

I learned of your absence
by heart.

The gold border
feels louder now,
and jealousy
feels heavier,
like a light left on for no one.

And I learned the hard way.

I'm healing, but your name still lives in my quiet.

I never expected to
make you, my habit.

But the notes margin
keeps showing up,
and my patience
doesn't know where to go.

It glowed
like chalk dust on fingertips.

And I waited without asking.

I’m moving on, and still—somewhere—I’m waiting.

I wore a smile outside
and broke in private.

Because of one
small thing:
the group photo.

It forgave
and I realised
I still carry gratitude
like a letter never posted.

And I acted normal.

I'm okay, but I still flinch at your absence.

I looked fine in public
and broke in private.

Because of one
small thing:
the assembly.

It glowed
and I realised
I still carry an ache
like stars behind city smoke.

And I smiled anyway.

I'm healing, but your name still lives in my quiet.

I laughed in crowded rooms
and broke in private.

Because of one
small thing:
Your hoodie.

It breathed
and I realised
I still carry relief
like the bell that already rang.

And I kept the secret.

I'm learning to breathe without erasing you.

I never planned to
make you, my habit.

But the last period
keeps showing up,
and my ache
doesn't know where to go.

It remembered
like a letter never posted.

And I looked away first.

I'm learning to breathe without erasing you.

You never belonged to me,
and still—

I learned of your absence
by heart.

Your hoodie
feels louder now,
and shame
feels heavier,
like a song fading mid-chorus.

And I kept the secret.

I'm learning to breathe without erasing you.

If loving you again
was a syllabus,
I studied it perfectly—
but the exam
was your indifference.

Now your
hoodie waited,
and I practice
letting go,

like chalk dust on fingertips.

And I kept the secret.

I'm not stuck—just faithful to what I felt.

You were never meant to be mine,
and still—

I learned of your absence
by heart.

The canteen table
feels louder now,
and patience
feels heavier,
like stars behind city smoke.

And I learned the hard way.

I let you go with open hands and an unfinished heart.

I never intended to
make you, my habit.

But the voice note
keeps showing up,
and my pride
doesn't know where to go.

It held
like a bruise you keep touching.

And I swallowed the truth.

Some loves end; some loves become part of you.

On restless nights
the group photo was released
in my mind,

like a bruise you keep touching.

I tell myself
it's just an ache,
not fate,

And I stayed quiet.

I'm learning to breathe without erasing you.

I wore a smile outside
and broke in private.

Because of one
small thing:
the matchstick spark.

It prayed
and I realised
I still carry patience
like a bruise you keep touching.

And I waited without asking.

I'm healing, but your name still lives in my quiet.

On certain nights
Your perfume disappeared
in my mind,

like a letter never posted.

I tell myself
it's just jealousy,
not fate,

And I chose myself—slowly.

Some loves end; some loves become part of you.

I looked fine in public
and broke in private.

Because of one
small thing:
the timetable.

It remembered
and I realised
I still carry shame
like chalk dust on fingertips.

And I forgave you in silence.

I'm healing, but your name still lives in my quiet.

If loving you once
was a syllabus,
I studied it perfectly—
But the exam
was your indifference.

Now the one
glance collapsed,
and I practice
letting go,

like stars behind city smoke.

And I kept the secret.

Some loves end; some loves become part of you.

I laughed in crowded rooms
and broke in private.

Because of one
small thing:
the group photo.

It rose
and I realised
I still carry regret
like a song fading mid-chorus.

And I let it pass.

I'm okay, but I still flinch at your absence.

At times
Your perfume rose
in my mind,

like the bell that already rang.

I tell myself
it's just confusion,
not fate,

And I swallowed the truth.

I'm okay, but I still flinch at your absence.

There are nights
the assembly rose
in my mind,

like perfume on a borrowed sweater.

I tell myself
it's just an ache,
not fate,

And I kept the secret.

I don't chase you anymore; my heart just remembers.

There are days
the timetable remembered
in my mind,

like a page torn carefully.

I tell myself
it's just softness,
not fate,

And I forgave you in silence.

I'm not stuck—just faithful to what I felt.

I never expected to
make you, my habit.

But the voice note
keeps showing up,
and my jealousy
doesn't know where to go.

It forgave
like laughter trapped in a throat.

And I let it pass.

I'm learning to breathe without erasing you.

I never planned to
make you, my habit.

But the seen at 2:13
keeps showing up,
and my shame
doesn't know where to go.

It pretended
like the last train leaving.

And I waited without asking.

I'm healing, but your name still lives in my quiet.

I wore a smile outside
and broke in private.

Because of one
small thing:
the school gate.

It drowned
and I realised
I still carry a longing
like a bruise you keep touching.

And I chose myself—slowly.

I don't chase you anymore; my heart just remembers.

I looked fine in public
and broke in private.

Because of one
small thing:
Your hoodie.

It disappeared
and I realised
I still carry quietly
like rain on warm concrete.

And I swallowed the truth.

I'm not stuck—just faithful to what I felt.

I never intended to
make you, my habit.

But the blue tick
keeps showing up,
and my hope
doesn't know where to go.

It remembered
like a light left on for no one.

And I waited without asking.

I'm okay, but I still flinch at your absence.

You were never truly mine,
and still—

I learned of your absence
by heart.

The assembly
feels louder now,
and faith
feels heavier,
like the last train leaving.

And I kept the secret.

I'm learning to breathe without erasing you.

I never expected to
make you, my habit.

But the notes margin
keeps showing up,
and my relief
doesn't know where to go.

It hesitated
like a bruise you keep touching.

And I swallowed the truth.

If you ever turn back, you'll find me softer, not smaller.

Every now and then
the classroom
window rewrote
in my mind,

like the last train leaving.

I tell myself
it's just quiet,
not fate,

And I kept the secret.

I'm not stuck—just faithful to what I felt.

If loving you at all
was a syllabus,
I studied it perfectly—
but the exam
was your indifference.

Now the classroom
window returned,
and I practice
letting go,

like the last train leaving.

And I waited without asking.

I love you enough to let you go—yet I still wait here.

I never planned to
make you, my habit.

But the matchstick spark
keeps showing up,
and my patience
doesn't know where to go.

It forgave
like rain on warm concrete.

And I chose myself—slowly.

Some loves end; some loves become part of you.

Once in a while
the exam season drowned
in my mind,

like a light left on for no one.

I tell myself
it's just hurt,
not fate,

And I waited without asking.

I'm healing, but your name still lives in my quiet.

You never belonged to me,
and still—

I learned of your absence
by heart.

The exam season
feels louder now,
and jealousy
feels heavier,
like stars behind city smoke.

And I acted normal.

I'm moving on, and still—somewhere—I'm waiting.

I never intended to
make you, my habit.

But the matchstick spark
keeps showing up,
and my panic
doesn't know where to go.

It collapsed
like a light left on for no one.

And I let it pass.

I'm learning to breathe without erasing you.

You were never meant to be mine,
and still—

I learned of your absence
by heart.

The late-night chat
feels louder now,
and panic
feels heavier,
like laughter trapped in a throat.

And I learned the hard way.

I'm okay, but I still flinch at your absence.

On restless nights
the song stuck waited
in my mind,

like stars behind city smoke.

I tell myself
it's just gratitude,
not fate,

And I kept the secret.

Some loves end; some loves become part of you.

If loving you again
was a syllabus,
I studied it perfectly—
but the exam
was your indifference.

Now your
perfume disappeared,
and I practice
letting go,

like rain on warm concrete.

And I waited without asking.

I'm learning to breathe without erasing you.

On certain nights
the inside joke played
in my mind,

like chalk dust on fingertips.

I tell myself
it's just longing,
not fate,

And I kept the secret.

I'm okay, but I still flinch at your absence.

At times
the inside joke was released
in my mind,

like a bruise you keep touching.

I tell myself
it's just dread,
not fate,

And I waited without asking.

Some loves end; some loves become part of you.

If loving you once
was a syllabus,
I studied it perfectly—
but the exam
was your indifference.

Now the seen at 2:13
returned, and I practice
letting go,

like the last train leaving.

And I learned the hard way.

Some loves end; some loves become part of you.

I laughed in crowded rooms
and broke in private.

Because of one
small thing:
the seen at 2:13.

It rose
and I realised
I still carry a longing
like stars behind city smoke.

And I forgave you in silence.

I'm not stuck—just faithful to what I felt.

On quiet days
the timetable lingered
in my mind,

like chalk dust on fingertips.

I tell myself
it's just panic,
not fate,

And I kept the secret.

I let you go with open hands and an unfinished heart.

If loving you at all
was a syllabus,
I studied it perfectly—
but the exam
was your indifference.

Now the seen at 2:13
disappeared, and I practice
letting go,

like a bruise you keep touching.

And I swallowed the truth.

Some loves end; some loves become part of you.

I wore a smile outside
and broke in private.

Because of one
small thing:
the rainy recess.

It disappeared
and I realized
I still carry quietly
like a bruise you keep touching.

And I waited without asking.

If you ever turn back, you'll find me softer, not smaller.

I never expected to
make you, my habit.

But the library's silence
keeps showing up,
and my calm
doesn't know where to go.

It waited
like chalk dust on fingertips.

And I forgave you in silence.

Some loves end; some loves become part of you.

If loving you again
was a syllabus,
I studied it perfectly—
but the exam
was your indifference.

Now the notes margin
shook, and I practice
letting go,

like laughter trapped in a throat.

And I smiled anyway.

Some loves end; some loves become part of you.

There are nights
Your laugh lingered
in my mind,

like a bruise you keep touching.

I tell myself
it's just tenderness,
not fate,

And I kept the secret.

I don't chase you anymore; my heart just remembers.

On restless nights
the assembly rose
in my mind,

like perfume on a borrowed sweater.

I tell myself
it's just hurt,
not fate,

And I chose myself—slowly.

I love you enough to let you go—yet I still wait here.

I never planned to
make you, my habit.

But the seen at 2:13
keeps showing up,
and my panic
doesn't know where to go.

It released
like rain on warm concrete.

And I smiled anyway.

I'm okay, but I still flinch at your absence.

On certain nights
the canteen table
shook in my mind,

like laughter trapped in a throat.

I tell myself
it's just hurt,
not fate,

And I looked away first.

I'm moving on, and still—somewhere—I'm waiting.

Every now and then
the one glance disappeared
in my mind,

like a letter never posted.

I tell myself
it's just panic,
not fate,

And I kept the secret.

I'm healing, but your name still lives in my quiet.

If loving you once
was a syllabus,
I studied it perfectly—
but the exam
was your indifference.

Now, the one glance
disappeared, and I practice
letting go,

like chalk dust on fingertips.

And I let it pass.

I don't chase you anymore; my heart just remembers.

I looked fine in public
and broke in private.

Because of one
small thing:
the voice note.

It stayed
and I realised
I still carry hope
like a light left on for no one.

And I acted normal.

I'm healing, but your name still lives in my quiet.

If loving you at all
was a syllabus,
I studied it perfectly—
but the exam
was your indifference.

Now the bus stop
collapsed, and I practice
letting go,

like stars behind city smoke.

And I swallowed the truth.

Some loves end; some loves become part of you.

Once in a while
the canteen table
remembered
in my mind,

like a letter never posted.

I tell myself
it’s just softness,
not fate,

And I stayed quiet.

I’m moving on, and still—somewhere—I’m waiting.

There are nights
the black saree
forgave in my mind,

like stars behind city smoke.

I tell myself
it's just shame,
not fate,

And I waited without asking.

I love you enough to let you go—yet I still wait here.

I laughed in crowded rooms
and broke in private.

Because of one
small thing:
the one glance.

It pretended
and I realised
I still carry regret
like perfume on a borrowed sweater.

And I smiled anyway.

I let you go with open hands and an unfinished heart.

I never intended to
make you, my habit.

But the assembly
keeps showing up,
and my longing
doesn't know where to go.

It unlearned
like the last train leaving.

And I looked away first.

If you ever turn back, you'll find me softer, not smaller.

If loving you again
was a syllabus,
I studied it perfectly—
but the exam
was your indifference.

Now the blue tick
held, and I practice
letting go,

Like the bell that already rang.

And I let it pass.

I'm learning to breathe without erasing you.

At times
the bus stop
remembered in my mind,

like a letter never posted.

I tell myself
it's just relief,
not fate,

And I chose myself—slowly.

I'm learning to breathe without erasing you.

I wore a smile outside
and broke in private.

Because of one
small thing:
the timetable.

It hesitated
and I realised
I still carry pride
like a bruise you keep touching.

And I swallowed the truth.

I don't chase you anymore; my heart just remembers.

You were never truly mine,
and still—

I learned of your absence
by heart.

The voice note
feels louder now,
and faith
feels heavier,
like a bruise you keep touching.

And I forgave you in silence.

If you ever turn back, you'll find me softer, not smaller.

On certain days
the rainy recess
waited in my mind,

like laughter trapped in a throat.

I tell myself
it's just confusion,
not fate,

And I looked away first.

I let you go with open hands and an unfinished heart.

I never expected to
make you, my habit.

But the song stuck
keeps showing up,
and my longing
doesn't know where to go.

It collapsed
like a bruise you keep touching.

And I smiled anyway.

Some loves end; some loves become part of you.

On restless nights
the staircase
released
in my mind,

like a letter never posted.

I tell myself
it's just jealousy,
not fate,

And I learned the hard way.

Some loves end; some loves become part of you.

You never belonged to me,
and still—

I learned of your absence
by heart.

The inside joke
feels louder now,
and calm
feels heavier,
like a light left on for no one.

And I chose myself—slowly.

I'm not stuck—just faithful to what I felt.

I never planned to
make you, my habit.

But the timetable
keeps showing up,
and my quiet
doesn't know where to go.

It breathed
like rain on warm concrete.

And I looked away first.

I let you go with open hands and an unfinished heart.

You were never meant to be mine,
and still—

I learned of your absence
by heart.

The one glance
feels louder now,
and softness
feels heavier,
like a letter never posted.

And I let it pass.

If you ever turn back, you'll find me softer, not smaller.

If loving you once
was a syllabus,
I studied it perfectly—
but the exam
was your indifference.

Now the canteen table
pretended, and I practice
letting go,

like a letter never posted.

And I chose myself—slowly.

I'm moving on, and still—somewhere—I'm waiting.

You were never truly mine,
and still—

I learned of your absence
by heart.

The corridor
feels louder now,
and dread
feels heavier,
like a page torn carefully.

And I kept the secret.

I'm not stuck—just faithful to what I felt.

There are days
the inside joke
stayed in my mind,

like a page torn carefully.

I tell myself
it's just hope,
not fate,

And I chose myself—slowly.

I'm learning to breathe without erasing you.

I looked fine in public
and broke in private.

Because of one
small thing:
the matchstick spark.

It collapsed
and I realised
I still carry hope
like the bell that already rang.

And I learned the hard way.

I don't chase you anymore; my heart just remembers.

You never belonged to me,
and still—

I learned of your absence
by heart.

The rainy recess
feels louder now,
and faith
feels heavier,
like a page torn carefully.

And I let it pass.

I'm not stuck—just faithful to what I felt.

I never intended to
make you, my habit.

But the gold border
keeps showing up,
and my quiet
doesn't know where to go.

It drowned
like a song fading mid-chorus.

And I acted normal.

I'm healing, but your name still lives in my quiet.

I laughed in crowded rooms
and broke in private.

Because of one
small thing:
the gold border.

It collapsed
and I realised
I still carry jealousy
like a light left on for no one.

And I swallowed the truth.

I'm learning to breathe without erasing you.

On certain nights
the library's silence
pretended in my mind,

like a light left on for no one.

I tell myself
it's just faith,
not fate,

And I stayed quiet.

I'm okay, but I still flinch at your absence.

I wore a smile outside
and broke in private.

Because of one
small thing:
the rainy recess.

It forgave
and I realised
I still carry softness
like perfume on a borrowed sweater.

And I waited without asking.

I'm moving on, and still—somewhere—I'm waiting.

On quiet days
the bus stop
lingered in my mind,

like rain on warm concrete.

I tell myself
it's just relief,
not fate,

And I wrote it down.

I'm moving on, and still—somewhere—I'm waiting.

You were never meant to be mine,
and still—

I learned of your absence
by heart.

The late-night chat
feels louder now,
and relief
feels heavier,
like a page torn carefully.

And I kept the secret.

I'm not stuck—just faithful to what I felt.

I never expected to
make you, my habit.

But the timetable
keeps showing up,
and my hope
doesn't know where to go.

It unfollowed
like the bell that already rang.

And I wrote it down.

I'm healing, but your name still lives in my quiet.

There are nights
the classroom window
shook in my mind,

like a letter never posted.

I tell myself
it's just pride,
not fate,

And I learned the hard way.

Some loves end; some loves become part of you.

You were never truly mine,
and still—

I learned of your absence
by heart.

The one glance
feels louder now,
and jealousy
feels heavier,
like chalk dust on fingertips.

And I swallowed the truth.

If you ever turn back, you'll find me softer, not smaller.

You never belonged to me,
and still—

I learned of your absence
by heart.

The canteen table
feels louder now,
and calm
feels heavier,
like a bruise you keep touching.

And I forgave you in silence.

I'm learning to breathe without erasing you.

I looked fine in public
and broke in private.

Because of one
small thing:
the timetable.

It returned
and I realised
I still carry regret
like laughter trapped in a throat.

And I looked away first.

I'm moving on, and still—somewhere—I'm waiting.

I laughed in crowded rooms
and broke in private.

Because of one
small thing:
The song stuck.

It collapsed
and I realised
I still carry tenderness
like a bruise you keep touching.

And I smiled anyway.

I don't chase you anymore; my heart just remembers.

You were never meant to be mine,
and still—

I learned of your absence
by heart.

The canteen table
feels louder now,
and regret
feels heavier,
like a song fading mid-chorus.

And I wrote it down.

I'm not stuck—just faithful to what I felt.

If loving you at all
was a syllabus,
I studied it perfectly—
But the exam
was your indifference.

Now the seen at 2:13
stayed, and I practice
letting go,

like a song fading mid-chorus.

And I learned the hard way.

If you ever turn back, you'll find me softer, not smaller.

I never planned to
make you, my habit.

But the bus stop
keeps showing up,
and my hurt
doesn't know where to go.

It rewrote
like laughter trapped in a throat.

And I forgave you in silence.

I'm healing, but your name still lives in my quiet.

I never intended to
make you, my habit.

But the timetable
keeps showing up,
and my panic
doesn't know where to go.

It waited
like rain on warm concrete.

And I looked away first.

I'm moving on, and still—somewhere—I'm waiting.

If loving you again
was a syllabus,
I studied it perfectly—
But the exam
was your indifference.

Now the gold border
stayed, and I practice
letting go,

like perfume on a borrowed sweater.

And I swallowed the truth.

I let you go with open hands and an unfinished heart.

You were never truly mine,
and still—

I learned of your absence
by heart.

The gold border
feels louder now,
and quiet
feels heavier,
like perfume on a borrowed sweater.

And I chose myself—slowly.

I'm moving on, and still—somewhere—I'm waiting.

I wore a smile outside
and broke in private.

Because of one
small thing:
the one glance.

It disappeared
and I realised
I still carry confusion
like stars behind city smoke.

And I smiled anyway.

I let you go with open hands and an unfinished heart.

If loving you once
was a syllabus,
I studied it perfectly—
But the exam
was your indifference.

Now the exam
season waited,
and I practice
letting go,

like the last train leaving.

And I acted normal.

Some loves end; some loves become part of you.

You never belonged to me,
and still—

I learned of your absence
by heart.

The assembly
feels louder now,
and relief
feels heavier,
like stars behind city smoke.

And I acted normal.

I love you enough to let you go—yet I still wait here.

If loving you at all
was a syllabus,
I studied it perfectly—
But the exam
was your indifference.

Now the song
stuck collapsed,
and I practice
letting go,

like perfume on a borrowed sweater.

And I smiled anyway.

I'm moving on, and still—somewhere—I'm waiting.

I looked fine in public
and broke in private.

Because of one
small thing:
the bus stop.

It remembered
and I realized
I still carry regret
like the last train leaving.

And I learned the hard way.

I love you enough to let you go—yet I still wait here.

I laughed in crowded rooms
and broke in private.

Because of one
small thing:
Your hoodie.

It rose
and I realised
I still carry quietly
like rain on warm concrete.

And I let it pass.

I'm moving on, and still—somewhere—I'm waiting.

Every now and then
the bus stop
lingered in my mind,

like stars behind city smoke.

I tell myself
it's just panic,
not fate,

And I smiled anyway.

Some loves end; some loves become part of you.

I wore a smile outside
and broke in private.

Because of one
small thing:
the exam season.

It lingered
and I realised
I still carry gratitude
like rain on warm concrete.

And I forgave you in silence.

I let you go with open hands and an unfinished heart.

You were never meant to be mine,
and still—

I learned of your absence
by heart.

The bus stop
feels louder now,
and shame
feels heavier,
like a page torn carefully.

And I let it pass.

Some loves end; some loves become part of you.

You were never truly mine,
and still—

I learned of your absence
by heart.

The classroom window
feels louder now,
and calm
feels heavier,
like perfume on a borrowed sweater.

And I chose myself—slowly.

I love you enough to let you go—yet I still wait here.

You never belonged to me,
and still—

I learned of your absence
by heart.

The assembly
feels louder now,
and confusion
feels heavier,
like a letter never posted.

And I waited without asking.

I'm learning to breathe without erasing you.

You were never meant to be mine,
and still—

I learned of your absence
by heart.

The blue tick
feels louder now,
and panic
feels heavier,
like a song fading mid-chorus.

And I chose myself—slowly.

I'm healing, but your name still lives in my quiet.

You were never truly mine,
and still—

I learned of your absence
by heart.

The unsent draft
feels louder now,
and regret
feels heavier,
like the last train leaving.

And I forgave you in silence.

If you ever turn back, you'll find me softer, not smaller.

Once in a while
the staircase rose
in my mind,

Like laughter trapped in a throat.

I tell myself
it's just regret,
not fate,

And I looked away first.

I'm okay, but I still flinch at your absence.

I stopped checking
if you still cared,

but my heart
still pauses
when your name appears.

Healing is strange —
Some doors close,
Yet memories stay open.

You were never mine,
and still,

every goodbye
felt personal.

Maybe some people
teach love,

just not forever.

I learned silence
because of you —

How to smile normally
while something inside
slowly, let's go.

Some endings
arrive quietly.

I let you go
without hatred,

only a soft hope
that life treats you well.

And somewhere,
between moving on
and remembering,

a part of me still waits.